This journal belongs to:

© 2011 by Barbour Publishing, Inc.

Compiled by Kathy Shutt.

ISBN 978-1-61626-184-9

Cover and interior design by Koechel Peterson & Associates, Minneapolis, Minnesota

Published by Barbour Publishing, Inc., P.O. Box 719, Uhrichsville, Ohio 44683,
www.barbourbooks.com

*Our mission is to publish and distribute inspirational products offering exceptional value and biblical
encouragement to the masses.*

 Member of the
Evangelical Christian
Publishers Association

Printed in China.

consider the lilies

a journal

BARBOUR
PUBLISHING

Consider the Lilies of the Field

The violets whisper from the shade
Which their own leaves have made:
Men scent our fragrance on the air,
Yet take no heed
Of humble lessons we would read.

But not alone the fairest flowers:
The merest grass
Along the roadside where we
pass. . .
Tell of His love who sends the dew,
The rain and sunshine too,
To nourish one small seed.

The violets whisper from the shade
Which their own leaves have made. . .

I would rather be able to appreciate
things I cannot have than to have
things I am not able to appreciate.

ELBERT HUBBARD

. . .Men scent our fragrance on the air,
Yet take no heed
Of humble lessons we would read.

When we take time to notice the simple things
in life, we never lack for encouragement.
We discover we are surrounded by limitless
hope that's just wearing everyday clothes.

Unknown

But not alone the fairest flowers:
The merest grass
Along the roadside where we pass. . .

Every moment is full of wonder
and God is always present.

UNKNOWN

. . .Tell of His love who sends the dew,
The rain and sunshine too,
To nourish one small seed.

Heavenly Father, You promise courage
and strength when I need them.
Thank You, Lord, for the hidden
strength You give me—Your strength.
Amen.

The violets whisper from the shade
Which their own leaves have made. . .

**"The eternal God is your refuge,
and underneath are the everlasting arms."**

DEUTERONOMY 33:27 NIV

. . .Men scent our fragrance on the air,
Yet take no heed
Of humble lessons we would read.

Enjoy the little things, for one day you may look back and discover they were the big things.
UNKNOWN

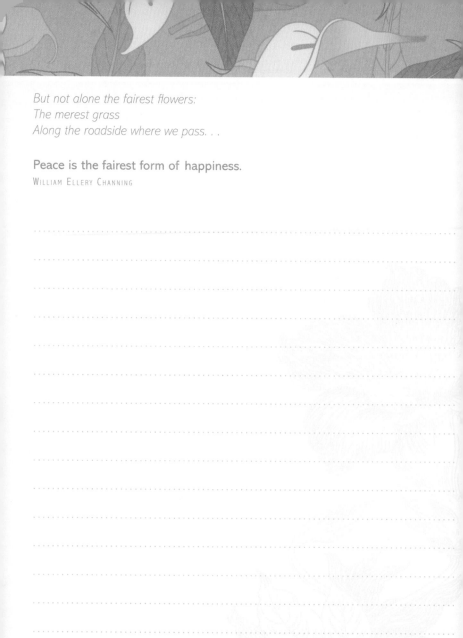

But not alone the fairest flowers:
The merest grass
Along the roadside where we pass. . .

Peace is the fairest form of happiness.
WILLIAM ELLERY CHANNING

. . .Tell of His love who sends the dew,
The rain and sunshine too,
To nourish one small seed.

Be faithful in little things,
for in them our strength lies.
MOTHER TERESA

The violets whisper from the shade
Which their own leaves have made. . .

Heavenly Father, when life seems to be getting rough, I pray, and the path becomes smooth before me. I know You have answered my prayer. Thank You for Your peace, which goes before me each day. Amen.

. . .Men scent our fragrance on the air,
Yet take no heed
Of humble lessons we would read.

You're my place of quiet retreat;
I wait for your Word to renew me. . .
therefore I lovingly embrace everything you say.

Psalm 119:114, 119 msg

But not alone the fairest flowers:
The merest grass
Along the roadside where we pass. . .

Life becomes a glorious experience of
discovering His endless wonders.

. . .Tell of His love who sends the dew,
The rain and sunshine too,
To nourish one small seed.

There's always something
to be thankful for.
CHARLES DICKENS

The violets whisper from the shade
Which their own leaves have made. . .

The best things are nearest: breath in your nostrils,
light in your eyes, flowers at your feet, duties at
your hand, the path of God just before you.

ROBERT LOUIS STEVENSON

. . .Men scent our fragrance on the air,
Yet take no heed
Of humble lessons we would read.

Thank You, Lord, for Your promise that if I am true to You,
You will take care of me, and I will produce good fruit.
What I cannot do on my own, You will accomplish,
if I trust in You. Amen.

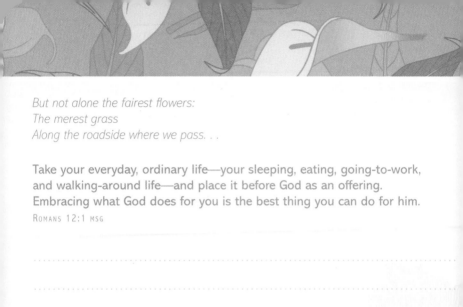

But not alone the fairest flowers:
The merest grass
Along the roadside where we pass. . .

Take your everyday, ordinary life—your sleeping, eating, going-to-work,
and walking-around life—and place it before God as an offering.
Embracing what God does for you is the best thing you can do for him.
ROMANS 12:1 MSG

. . .Tell of His love who sends the dew,
The rain and sunshine too,
To nourish one small seed.

The serene have not opted out of life.
They see things more widely, love more dearly,
rejoice in the things the frantic mind no longer sees or hears.

PAM BROWN

The violets whisper from the shade
Which their own leaves have made. . .

Don't judge each day by the harvest you reap but by the seeds that you plant.
ROBERT LOUIS STEVENSON

. . .Men scent our fragrance on the air,
Yet take no heed
Of humble lessons we would read.

Wherever God dwells, there is heaven.

Teresa of Avila

But not alone the fairest flowers:
The merest grass
Along the roadside where we pass. . .

Fill me with Your Spirit, Lord, so that I may glorify You in every choice I make. Amen.

. . .Tell of His love who sends the dew,
The rain and sunshine too,
To nourish one small seed.

"Oh, that we might know the LORD!
Let us press on to know him. He will respond
to us as surely as the arrival of dawn or the
coming of rains in early spring."

HOSEA 6:3 NLT

The violets whisper from the shade
Which their own leaves have made. . .

To think of [God's] rest is to give rest to the soul.
BERNARD OF CLAIRVAUX

. . .Men scent our fragrance on the air,
Yet take no heed
Of humble lessons we would read.

**A gentle word, a kind look, a good-natured smile
can work wonders and accomplish miracles.**
WILLIAM HAZLITT

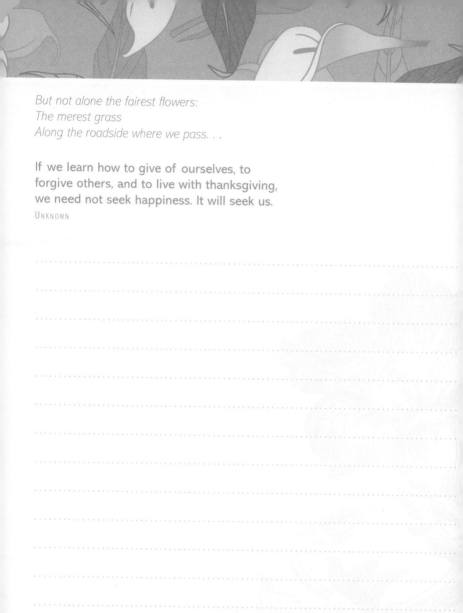

But not alone the fairest flowers:
The merest grass
Along the roadside where we pass. . .

If we learn how to give of ourselves, to
forgive others, and to live with thanksgiving,
we need not seek happiness. It will seek us.

UNKNOWN

. . .Tell of His love who sends the dew,
The rain and sunshine too,
To nourish one small seed.

You have not only promised today's salvation, Lord,
but an eternity of life with You. When doubts assail,
increase my hope. Help me to wait patiently for
that final salvation. My hope lies in You alone. Amen.

The violets whisper from the shade
Which their own leaves have made. . .

May the God of hope fill you with all
joy and peace as you trust in him,
so that you may overflow with hope
by the power of the Holy Spirit.

ROMANS 15:13 NIV

. . .Men scent our fragrance on the air,
Yet take no heed
Of humble lessons we would read.

My greatest wealth is the deep stillness in which
I strive and grow and win what the world cannot
take from me with fire and sword.

JOHANN WOLFGANG VON GOETHE

But not alone the fairest flowers:
The merest grass
Along the roadside where we pass. . .

Doing little things with a strong desire
to please God makes them really great.

FRANCIS DE SALES

. . .Tell of His love who sends the dew,
The rain and sunshine too,
To nourish one small seed.

I rest on the Rock, and the Rock holds me,
Resting on the Rock of God.

Mrs. C. Rice

The violets whisper from the shade
Which their own leaves have made. . .

Keep me obedient to Your love, Lord.
Help me trust that You will bring me good things.
I need faith to see blessings instead of fears.
Amen.

. . .Men scent our fragrance on the air,
Yet take no heed
Of humble lessons we would read.

But those who trust in the LORD **will find new strength.**
They will soar high on wings like eagles.
ISAIAH 40:31 NLT

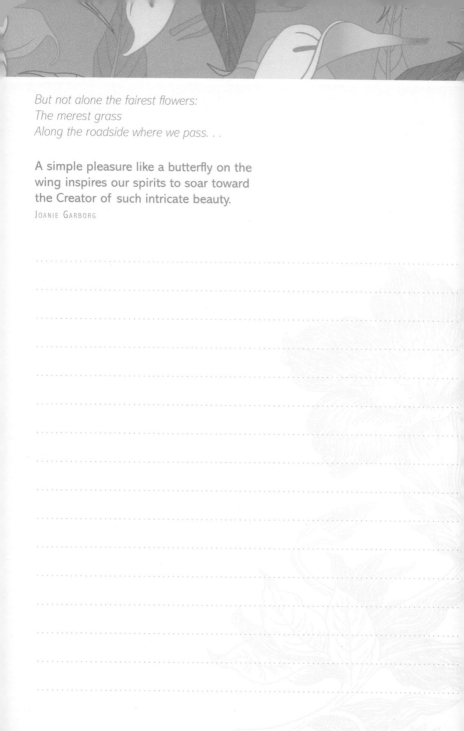

But not alone the fairest flowers:
The merest grass
Along the roadside where we pass. . .

A simple pleasure like a butterfly on the
wing inspires our spirits to soar toward
the Creator of such intricate beauty.

JOANIE GARBORG

. . .Tell of His love who sends the dew,
The rain and sunshine too,
To nourish one small seed.

Resolve to see the world on the sunny side,
and you have almost won the battle of life at the outset.

Sir Roger L'Estrange

The violets whisper from the shade
Which their own leaves have made. . .

Go out into the darkness and put
your hand into the hand of God.
That shall be to you better light
and safer than a known way.

MINNIE LOUISE HASKINS

. . .Men scent our fragrance on the air,
Yet take no heed
Of humble lessons we would read.

Although I cannot physically touch Your hand, I can feel Your presence, Your desire to protect and guide me. Thank You, Lord, for always staying close. Amen.

But not alone the fairest flowers:
The merest grass
Along the roadside where we pass. . .

Take my yoke upon you, and learn of me. . .
and ye shall find rest unto your souls.
MATTHEW 11:29 KJV

. . .Tell of His love who sends the dew,
The rain and sunshine too,
To nourish one small seed.

If the day and the night are such that
you greet them with joy, and life emits a
fragrance like flowers and sweet-scented
herbs, is more elastic, more starry,
more immortal—that is your success.

HENRY DAVID THOREAU

The violets whisper from the shade
Which their own leaves have made. . .

Live today fully, expressing gratitude for all you have
been, all you are right now, and all you are becoming.
MELODIE BEATTIE

. . .Men scent our fragrance on the air,
Yet take no heed
Of humble lessons we would read.

Teach me the art of creating islands of stillness,
in which I can absorb the beauty of everyday things:
clouds, trees, a snatch of music. . . .

MARION STROUD

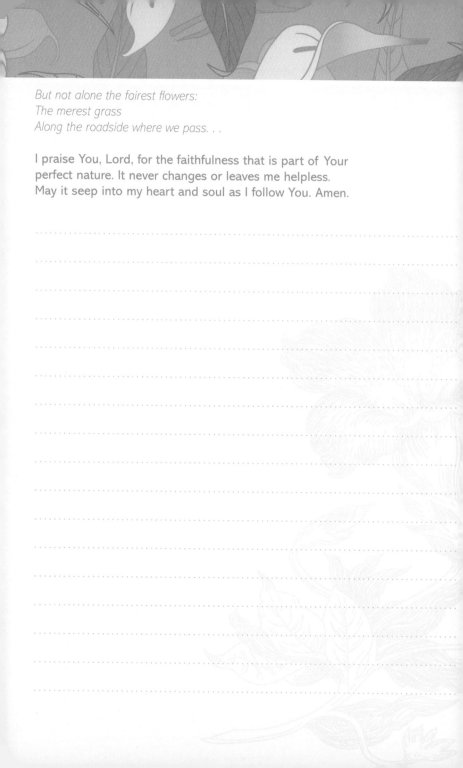

But not alone the fairest flowers:
The merest grass
Along the roadside where we pass. . .

I praise You, Lord, for the faithfulness that is part of Your
perfect nature. It never changes or leaves me helpless.
May it seep into my heart and soul as I follow You. Amen.

. . .Tell of His love who sends the dew,
The rain and sunshine too,
To nourish one small seed.

Casting all your care upon him;
for he careth for you.
1 PETER 5:7 KJV

The violets whisper from the shade
Which their own leaves have made. . .

Always begin anew with the day,
just as nature does; it is one of the
sensible things that nature does.
GEORGE E. WOODBERRY

. . .Men scent our fragrance on the air,
Yet take no heed
Of humble lessons we would read.

I can see how it might be possible for a man to
look down upon the earth and be an atheist,
but I cannot conceive how he could look up into
the heavens and say there is no God.

But not alone the fairest flowers:
The merest grass
Along the roadside where we pass. . .

Everything received with gratitude;
everything passed on with grace.

G. K. CHESTERTON

. . .Tell of His love who sends the dew,
The rain and sunshine too,
To nourish one small seed.

Thank You, Father God, for not only saving
me through Your Son, Jesus, but for giving
me Your power to make each day count for
You. Help me not to leave Your Spirit on the
shelf but to make Him a part
of my life always. Amen.

The violets whisper from the shade
Which their own leaves have made. . .

Whatsoever things are lovely. . .
think on these things.

PHILIPPIANS 4:8 KJV

. . .Men scent our fragrance on the air,
Yet take no heed
Of humble lessons we would read.

Allow yourself some time for silence.
Simply being before God will regenerate your spirit.
<small>UNKNOWN</small>

But not alone the fairest flowers:
The merest grass
Along the roadside where we pass. . .

There are two ways to live your life. One is as though nothing is a miracle. The other is as though everything is miracle.
ALBERT EINSTEIN

. . .Tell of His love who sends the dew,
The rain and sunshine too,
To nourish one small seed.

Calm me, O Lord, as you still the storm;
Still me, O Lord; keep me from harm.
Let all the tumult within me cease;
Enfold me, Lord, in your peace.

CELTIC PRAYER

*The violets whisper from the shade
Which their own leaves have made. . .*

Your kingdom, Father, is better than
this world could ever be. I want to
be an active part of it. Amen.

....
....
....
....
....
....
....
....
....
....
....
....
....
....
....
....
....
....

. . .Men scent our fragrance on the air,
Yet take no heed
Of humble lessons we would read.

"Be still, and know that I am God."
PSALM 46:10 NIV

But not alone the fairest flowers:
The merest grass
Along the roadside where we pass. . .

Keep your face upturned to [God] as
the flowers do to the sun.

HANNAH WHITALL SMITH

. . .Tell of His love who sends the dew,
The rain and sunshine too,
To nourish one small seed.

There is no season such delight can bring,
As summer, autumn, winter and spring.

WILLIAM BROWNE

The violets whisper from the shade
Which their own leaves have made. . .

An instant of pure love is more precious to God. . .
than all other good works together,
even though it may seem as if nothing were done.

JOHN OF THE CROSS

. . .Men scent our fragrance on the air,
Yet take no heed
Of humble lessons we would read.

Thank You, Lord, for leading me to do good things and then allowing me to reap the harvest of blessings that comes with them. I ask for nothing, but You give me everything I could ever hope for and will never deserve. Amen.

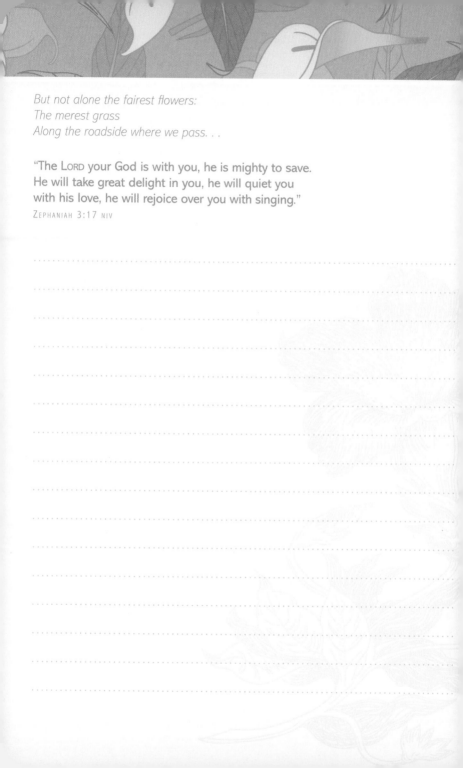

But not alone the fairest flowers:
The merest grass
Along the roadside where we pass. . .

"The Lord your God is with you, he is mighty to save.
He will take great delight in you, he will quiet you
with his love, he will rejoice over you with singing."
Zephaniah 3:17 NIV

. . .Tell of His love who sends the dew,
The rain and sunshine too,
To nourish one small seed.

A simple pleasure like an evening on the front porch
opens our hearts to love our neighbors as ourselves.

JOANIE GARBORG

The violets whisper from the shade
Which their own leaves have made. . .

The consciousness of loving and being loved brings a warmth and richness to life that nothing else can bring.
OSCAR WILDE

. . .Men scent our fragrance on the air,
Yet take no heed
Of humble lessons we would read.

Our greatest experiences
are our quietest moments.

FRIEDRICH NIETZSCHE

But not alone the fairest flowers:
The merest grass
Along the roadside where we pass. . .

Thank You, Lord, for lifting my heart
in joy when I think of Your salvation.
Amen.

. . .Tell of His love who sends the dew,
The rain and sunshine too,
To nourish one small seed.

Do not conform any longer to the
pattern of this world, but be transformed
by the renewing of your mind.

ROMANS 12:2 NIV

The violets whisper from the shade
Which their own leaves have made. . .

**Cheerfulness brings sunshine to the soul and
drives away the shadows of anxiety.**

HANNAH WHITALL SMITH

. . .Men scent our fragrance on the air,
Yet take no heed
Of humble lessons we would read.

Earth with her thousand voices praises God.

Samuel Taylor Coleridge

But not alone the fairest flowers:
The merest grass
Along the roadside where we pass. . .

Blue skies with white clouds on summer days. A myriad of stars on clear moonlit nights. Tulips and roses and violets and dandelions and daisies. Bluebirds and laughter and sunshine and Easter. See how [God] loves us!

ALICE CHAPIN

. . .Tell of His love who sends the dew,
The rain and sunshine too,
To nourish one small seed.

You, Lord, provide me with a lifetime of insight for
leading a life that glorifies You and makes me more
like You. Help me live every moment by the light of
Your Word and become righteous through knowledge
of Your Son, Jesus Christ. Amen.

The violets whisper from the shade
Which their own leaves have made. . .

"Steep yourself in God-reality, God-initiative, God-provisions. You'll find all your everyday human concerns will be met."
LUKE 12:30–31 MSG

. . . .

. . . .

. . . .

. . . .

. . . .

. . . .

. . . .

. . . .

. . . .

. . . .

. . . .

. . . .

. . . .

. . . .

. . . .

. . . .

. . .Men scent our fragrance on the air,
Yet take no heed
Of humble lessons we would read.

When prayer is at its highest, we wait in silence for
God's voice to us; we linger in His presence for His
peace and His power to flow over us and around us;
we lean back in His everlasting arms and feel the
serenity of perfect security in Him.

WILLIAM BARCLAY

But not alone the fairest flowers:
The merest grass
Along the roadside where we pass. . .

**Life finds its noblest spring of excellence
in this hidden impulse to do our best.**

ROBERT COLLYER

. . .Tell of His love who sends the dew,
The rain and sunshine too,
To nourish one small seed.

Serenity and inner beauty come
when we wait upon God.
EVA BURROWS

The violets whisper from the shade
Which their own leaves have made. . .

Help me trust in Your great plan for my life, Lord.
Show me Your will, and I will follow it, because
I know that trusting You will bring a future more
wonderful than I can imagine. Amen.

. . .Men scent our fragrance on the air,
Yet take no heed
Of humble lessons we would read.

But the path of the just is as the shining light,
that shineth more and more unto the perfect day.

PROVERBS 4:18 KJV

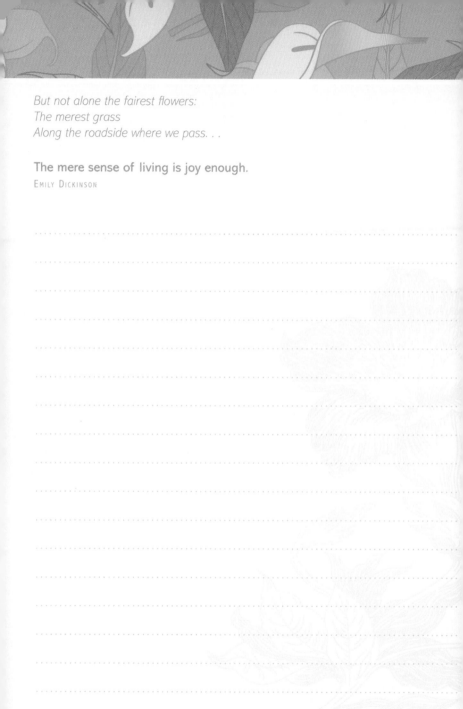

But not alone the fairest flowers:
The merest grass
Along the roadside where we pass. . .

The mere sense of living is joy enough.

EMILY DICKINSON

. . .Tell of His love who sends the dew,
The rain and sunshine too,
To nourish one small seed.

God's hand is always there;
once you grasp it, He'll never let go.
UNKNOWN

The violets whisper from the shade
Which their own leaves have made. . .

All things bright and beautiful,
all creatures great and small,
All things wise and wonderful,
the Lord God made them all.

CECIL FRANCES ALEXANDER

. . .Men scent our fragrance on the air,
Yet take no heed
Of humble lessons we would read.

Only when my life is anchored in Your love
will my joy endure regardless of the
circumstances. And that's the kind of joy I
want—steady and enduring. Thank You,
Lord, for a heart full of divine joy. Amen.

But not alone the fairest flowers:
The merest grass
Along the roadside where we pass. . .

**Surely goodness and love will follow
me all the days of my life.**

PSALM 23:6 NIV

. . .Tell of His love who sends the dew,
The rain and sunshine too,
To nourish one small seed.

God. . .still shines a beacon and a hope.

HERMAN MELVILLE

The violets whisper from the shade
Which their own leaves have made. . .

The sun. . .in its full glory, either at rising or setting—
this and many other like blessings we enjoy daily;
and for the most of them, because they are so common,
most men forget to pay their praises. But let us not.

IZAAK WALTON

. . . .

. . . .

. . . .

. . . .

. . . .

. . . .

. . . .

. . . .

. . . .

. . . .

. . . .

. . . .

. . . .

. . . .

. . .Men scent our fragrance on the air,
Yet take no heed
Of humble lessons we would read.

Yesterday is gone. Tomorrow has not yet come.
We only have today. Let us begin.
MOTHER TERESA

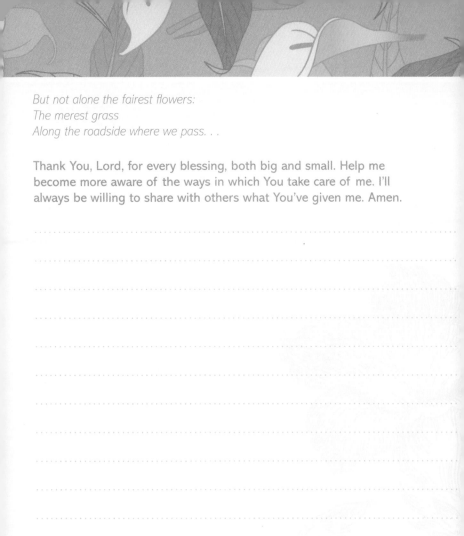

But not alone the fairest flowers:
The merest grass
Along the roadside where we pass. . .

Thank You, Lord, for every blessing, both big and small. Help me become more aware of the ways in which You take care of me. I'll always be willing to share with others what You've given me. Amen.

. . .Tell of His love who sends the dew,
The rain and sunshine too,
To nourish one small seed.

He. . .crowns me with love and tender mercies.
He fills my life with good things.

PSALM 103:4–5 NLT

The violets whisper from the shade
Which their own leaves have made. . .

From the simplest seeds of childlike
faith, we reap the lovely harvest of
God's reassuring presence in our lives.
UNKNOWN

. . .Men scent our fragrance on the air,
Yet take no heed
Of humble lessons we would read.

This life is not all. It is an "unfinished
symphony". . .with those who know
that they are related to God and have
felt "the power of an endless life."

HENRY WARD BEECHER

But not alone the fairest flowers:
The merest grass
Along the roadside where we pass. . .

God. . .wraps Himself in the splendor of the sun's light and walks among the clouds.

. . .Tell of His love who sends the dew,
The rain and sunshine too,
To nourish one small seed.

Thank You for my life, Lord. Every breath I
breathe is a gift from You. My beating heart,
my pulsing blood, eyes that see, and fingers
that can touch the ones I love. Amen.

The violets whisper from the shade
Which their own leaves have made. . .

And we know that all things work together
for good to them that love God, to them who
are the called according to his purpose.

ROMANS 8:28 KJV

. . .Men scent our fragrance on the air,
Yet take no heed
Of humble lessons we would read.

When I think upon my God, my heart is so full of
joy that the notes dance and leap from my pen.

Franz Josef Haydn

But not alone the fairest flowers:
The merest grass
Along the roadside where we pass. . .

Half the joy of life is in the little things taken on the run. Let us run
if we must. . .but let us keep our hearts young and our eyes open
that nothing worth our while shall escape us. And everything is
worth its while if we only grasp it and its significance.

CHARLES VICTOR CERBULIEZ

. . .Tell of His love who sends the dew,
The rain and sunshine too,
To nourish one small seed.

I often think flowers are the angels' alphabet
whereby they write on hills and fields mysterious
and beautiful lessons for us to feel and learn.

Louisa May Alcott

The violets whisper from the shade
Which their own leaves have made. . .

I am Your beloved child, Father, and You take great pleasure in giving me good things when I ask in faith. Thank You, Lord. Amen.

. . . .

. . . .

. . . .

. . . .

. . . .

. . . .

. . . .

. . . .

. . . .

. . . .

. . . .

. . . .

. . . .

. . . .

. . . .

. . . .

. . .Men scent our fragrance on the air,
Yet take no heed
Of humble lessons we would read.

He will cover you with his feathers, and under
his wings you will find refuge; his faithfulness
will be your shield and rampart.

PSALM 91:4 NIV

But not alone the fairest flowers:
The merest grass
Along the roadside where we pass. . .

All I want is to stand in a field
and to smell green, to taste the air,
to feel the earth. . .

PHILLIP PULFREY

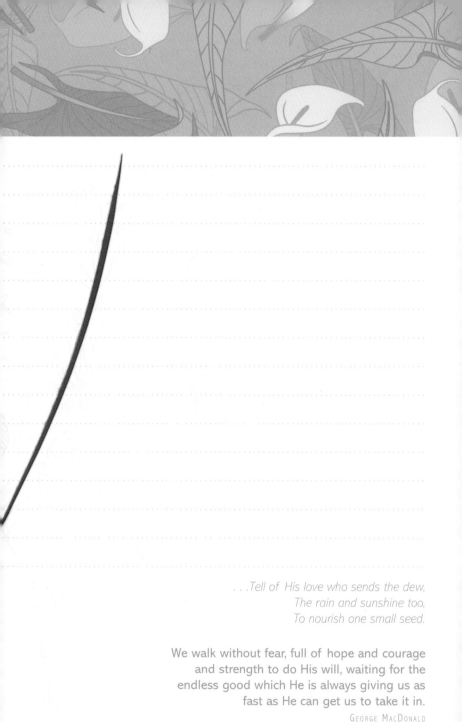

. . .Tell of His love who sends the dew,
The rain and sunshine too,
To nourish one small seed.

We walk without fear, full of hope and courage
and strength to do His will, waiting for the
endless good which He is always giving us as
fast as He can get us to take it in.

GEORGE MacDONALD

The violets whisper from the shade
Which their own leaves have made. . .

Always remember to forget the things that
made you sad. But never forget to remember
the things that made you glad.

ELBERT HUBBARD

. . .Men scent our fragrance on the air,
Yet take no heed
Of humble lessons we would read.

Whether or not I am seeking rewards You promised,
Lord, I know You provide good things for me.
Help me to seek You in faith for all my needs. Amen.

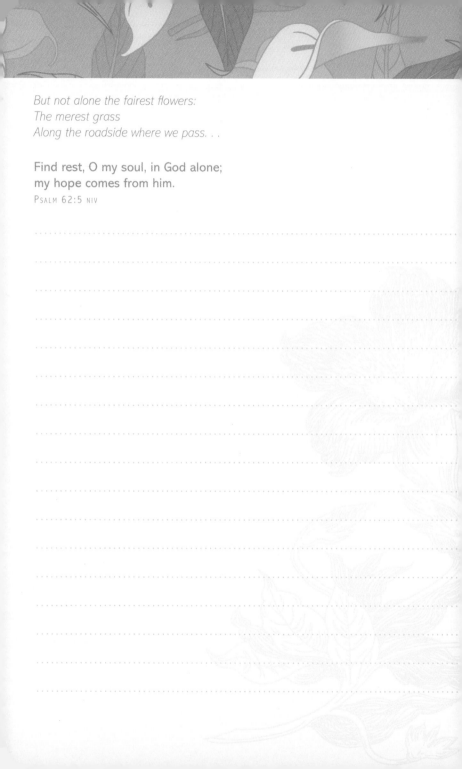

But not alone the fairest flowers:
The merest grass
Along the roadside where we pass. . .

Find rest, O my soul, in God alone;
my hope comes from him.

PSALM 62:5 NIV

. . .Tell of His love who sends the dew,
The rain and sunshine too,
To nourish one small seed.

The private and personal blessings we enjoy. . .
deserve the thanksgiving of a whole life.

JEREMY TAYLOR

The violets whisper from the shade
Which their own leaves have made. . .

Love makes burdens lighter because you divide them. It makes joys more intense because you share them. It makes you stronger so that you can reach out and become involved with life in ways you dared not risk alone.

Unknown

. . . .

. . . .

. . . .

. . . .

. . . .

. . . .

. . . .

. . . .

. . . .

. . . .

. . . .

. . . .

. . . .

. . .Men scent our fragrance on the air,
Yet take no heed
Of humble lessons we would read.

Be it ours, when we cannot see the face of God,
to trust under the shadow of His wings.

<small>CHARLES SPURGEON</small>

But not alone the fairest flowers:
The merest grass
Along the roadside where we pass. . .

What you promise, Father. I may not
always be faithful, but You always are.
I know I can trust You. Amen.

. . .Tell of His love who sends the dew,
The rain and sunshine too,
To nourish one small seed.

"You know with all your heart and soul
that not one of all the good promises
the LORD your God gave you has failed.
Every promise has been fulfilled."

JOSHUA 23:14 NIV

The violets whisper from the shade
Which their own leaves have made. . .

This is my Father's world:
I rest me in the thought
Of rocks and trees, of skies and seas;
His hand the wonders wrought.

MALTBIE D. BABCOCK

. . .Men scent our fragrance on the air,
Yet take no heed
Of humble lessons we would read.

All men who love with any degree of
serenity live by some assurance of grace.
REINHOLD NIEBUHR

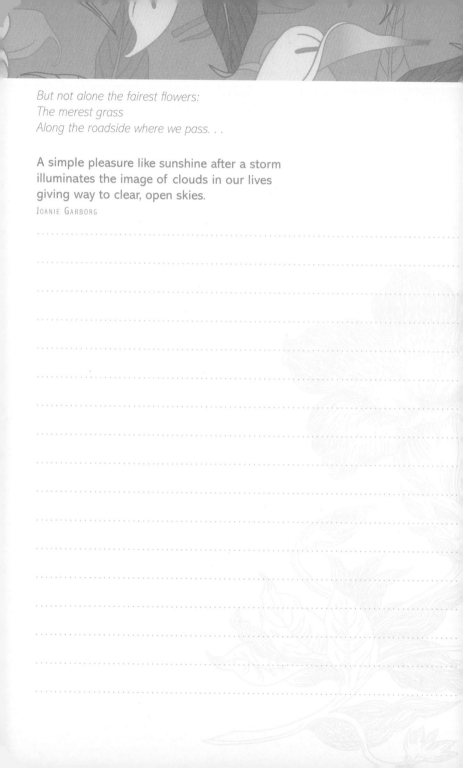

But not alone the fairest flowers:
The merest grass
Along the roadside where we pass. . .

A simple pleasure like sunshine after a storm
illuminates the image of clouds in our lives
giving way to clear, open skies.

JOANIE GARBORG

. . .Tell of His love who sends the dew,
The rain and sunshine too,
To nourish one small seed.

Heavenly Father, compared to the rest of the world, I am
rich and living a good life. Keep me mindful of my blessings,
no matter how much or little I have. Encourage me to use
what I have in a way that brings glory to You. Amen.

The violets whisper from the shade
Which their own leaves have made. . .

"Peace I leave with you; my peace I
give you. I do not give to you as the
world gives. Do not let your hearts
be troubled and do not be afraid."
JOHN 14:27 NIV

. . .Men scent our fragrance on the air,
Yet take no heed
Of humble lessons we would read.

A simple grateful thought toward
heaven is the most perfect prayer.
G. E. Lessing

But not alone the fairest flowers:
The merest grass
Along the roadside where we pass. . .

Only God gives true peace—a quiet gift He sets within us.

UNKNOWN

. . .Tell of His love who sends the dew,
The rain and sunshine too,
To nourish one small seed.

Our Creator would never have made such
lovely days, and have given us the deep hearts
to enjoy them, above and beyond all thought,
unless we were meant to be immortal.

NATHANIEL HAWTHORNE

The violets whisper from the shade
Which their own leaves have made. . .

Some people, in order to discover God, read books.
But there is a great book: the very appearance of
created things. Look above you! Look below you!

St. Augustine

. . .Men scent our fragrance on the air,
Yet take no heed
Of humble lessons we would read.

For God, who said, "Let light shine out of darkness,"
made his light shine in our hearts to give us the light of
the knowledge of the glory of God in the face of Christ.

2 CORINTHIANS 4:6 NIV

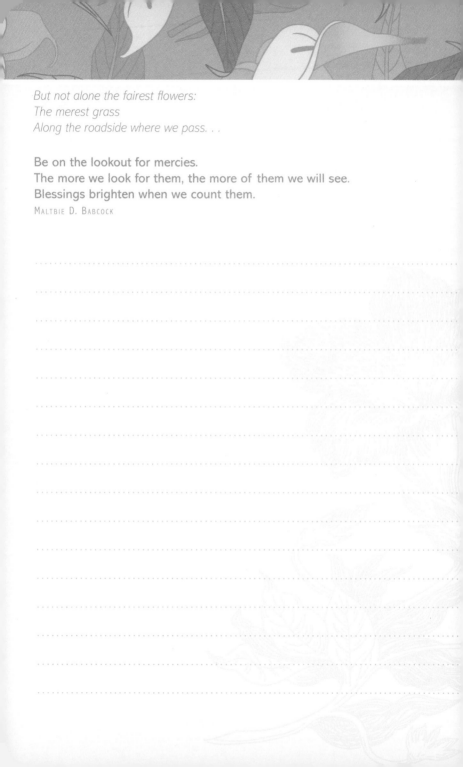

But not alone the fairest flowers:
The merest grass
Along the roadside where we pass. . .

Be on the lookout for mercies.
The more we look for them, the more of them we will see.
Blessings brighten when we count them.
MALTBIE D. BABCOCK

. . .Tell of His love who sends the dew,
The rain and sunshine too,
To nourish one small seed.

We are born to have connection with God.
Clement of Alexandria

The violets whisper from the shade
Which their own leaves have made. . .

Grace turns lions into lambs,
wolves into sheep, monsters into men,
and men into angels.
THOMAS CARLYLE

. . .Men scent our fragrance on the air,
Yet take no heed
Of humble lessons we would read.

I am only a tiny speck of light in a dark world,
Lord, but You promise that will be more than
enough. All power and glory are Yours. Amen.

But not alone the fairest flowers:
The merest grass
Along the roadside where we pass. . .

Submit yourselves, then, to God. . . .
Come near to God and he
will come near to you.

JAMES 4:7–8 NIV

. . .Tell of His love who sends the dew,
The rain and sunshine too,
To nourish one small seed.

The soul should always stand ajar,
ready to welcome the ecstatic experience.

EMILY DICKINSON

The violets whisper from the shade
Which their own leaves have made. . .

Drop thy still dews of quietness,
Till all our strivings cease;
Take from our souls the strain and stress,
And let our ordered lives confess
The beauty of thy peace.

JOHN G. WHITTIER

. . .Men scent our fragrance on the air,
Yet take no heed
Of humble lessons we would read.

The year's at the spring and days at the morn. . . .
God's in His heaven—all's right with the world!

ROBERT BROWNING

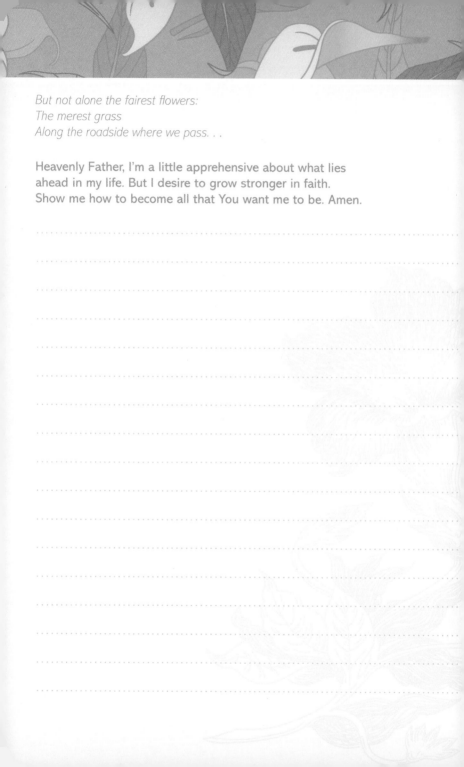

But not alone the fairest flowers:
The merest grass
Along the roadside where we pass. . .

Heavenly Father, I'm a little apprehensive about what lies
ahead in my life. But I desire to grow stronger in faith.
Show me how to become all that You want me to be. Amen.

. . .Tell of His love who sends the dew,
The rain and sunshine too,
To nourish one small seed.

[God] restores my soul.
PSALM 23:3 NIV

The violets whisper from the shade
Which their own leaves have made. . .

I long for scenes where man has never trod; A place where woman never smil'd or wept; There to abide with my creator, God.

JOHN CLARE

. . .Men scent our fragrance on the air,
Yet take no heed
Of humble lessons we would read.

All the beautiful sentiments in the world weigh
less than a simple lovely action.
JAMES RUSSELL LOWELL

But not alone the fairest flowers:
The merest grass
Along the roadside where we pass. . .

While our hearts are pure,
Our lives are happy and
our peace is sure.

WILLIAM WINTER

. . .Tell of His love who sends the dew,
The rain and sunshine too,
To nourish one small seed.

Help me, Lord, to focus on all You've given
me—blessings that transcend earthly
possessions. Help me recognize each gift
with a heart filled with gratitude. Amen.

The violets whisper from the shade
Which their own leaves have made. . .

My soul will rejoice in the LORD
and delight in his salvation.
PSALM 35:9 NIV

. . .Men scent our fragrance on the air,
Yet take no heed
Of humble lessons we would read.

Jesus—Light of the world. Joy of our hearts.
UNKNOWN

But not alone the fairest flowers:
The merest grass
Along the roadside where we pass. . .

A thing of beauty is a joy forever:
Its loveliness increases; it will never
Pass into nothingness.
JOHN KEATS

. . .Tell of His love who sends the dew,
The rain and sunshine too,
To nourish one small seed.

There is springtime in my soul today,
For, when the Lord is near,
The dove of peace sings in my heart,
The flowers of grace appear.

ELIZA HEWITT

The violets whisper from the shade
Which their own leaves have made. . .

Birds sing after a storm; why shouldn't people feel as free to delight in whatever remains to them?
Rose F. Kennedy

. . .Men scent our fragrance on the air,
Yet take no heed
Of humble lessons we would read.

Love never gives up, never loses faith, is
always hopeful, and endures through every
circumstance. . . . Love will last forever!

1 CORINTHIANS 13:7–8 NLT

But not alone the fairest flowers:
The merest grass
Along the roadside where we pass. . .

Wishing you all the simple
pleasures in life and the time
in which to enjoy them.

UNKNOWN

. . .Tell of His love who sends the dew,
The rain and sunshine too,
To nourish one small seed.

I thank You, God, for this most amazing day, for
the leaping greenly spirits of trees,
and for the blue dream of sky and for everything
which is natural, which is infinite, which is yes.

E. E. CUMMINGS

The violets whisper from the shade
Which their own leaves have made. . .

God loves us, and the will of love
is always blessing for its loved ones.

HANNAH WHITALL SMITH

. . .Men scent our fragrance on the air,
Yet take no heed
Of humble lessons we would read.

Father, teach me to trust that You know what's best for
me and that You are holding me in the palm of Your hand.
Thank You for the peace that passes all understanding—
the peace that knows my future is safe with You. Amen.

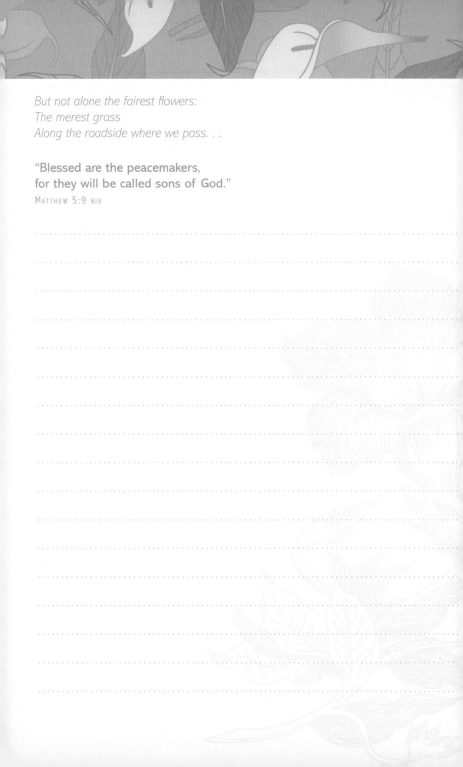

But not alone the fairest flowers:
The merest grass
Along the roadside where we pass. . .

"Blessed are the peacemakers,
for they will be called sons of God."
MATTHEW 5:9 NIV

. . .Tell of His love who sends the dew,
The rain and sunshine too,
To nourish one small seed.

Contentment is not the fulfillment of what you want,
but the realization of how much you already have.

UNKNOWN

*The violets whisper from the shade
Which their own leaves have made. . .*

**The patterns of our days are always
changing. . .rearranging. . .and each
design for living is unique. . .graced
with its own beauty.**
UNKNOWN

. . . .

. . . .

. . . .

. . . .

. . . .

. . . .

. . . .

. . . .

. . . .

. . . .

. . . .

. . . .

. . . .

. . . .

. . . .

. . .Men scent our fragrance on the air,
  Yet take no heed
  Of humble lessons we would read.

Every encounter, every incident during the day
is grist for the mill of the ongoing God-human
communication. No activity is too small or too
unimportant to meditate the holy.

NORVENE VEST

But not alone the fairest flowers:
The merest grass
Along the roadside where we pass. . .

Lord God, my faith in You is not based
in my senses or my intellect but in Your
never-failing love. Amen.

. . .Tell of His love who sends the dew,
The rain and sunshine too,
To nourish one small seed.

"The Counselor, the Holy Spirit, whom
the Father will send in my name, will
teach you all things and will remind
you of everything I have said to you."

JOHN 14:26 NIV

The violets whisper from the shade
Which their own leaves have made. . .

Do a deed of simple kindness;
Though its end you may not see,
It may reach, like a widening ripple,
Down a long eternity.

JOSEPH PARKER NORRIS

. . .Men scent our fragrance on the air,
Yet take no heed
Of humble lessons we would read.

Lasting peace of mind is impossible apart from peace
with God, yet enduring peace with God comes only when
a man is ready to surrender his own peace of mind.

A. ROY ECKARDT

But not alone the fairest flowers:
The merest grass
Along the roadside where we pass. . .

**The simplest and commonest truth seems
new and wonderful when we experience it
for the first time in our own life.**
<small>MARIE VON EBNER-ESCHENBACH</small>

. . . .

. . . .

. . . .

. . . .

. . . .

. . . .

. . . .

. . . .

. . . .

. . . .

. . . .

. . . .

. . . .

. . . .

. . . .

. . . .

. . .Tell of His love who sends the dew,
The rain and sunshine too,
To nourish one small seed.

Lord, help me forget the cares of the world for today;
fill my heart with light as Your blessings fall upon
me and I grow closer to You. Amen.

The violets whisper from the shade
Which their own leaves have made. . .

Come to me, all you that are weary
and are carrying heavy burdens,
and I will give you rest.
MATTHEW 11:28 NRSV

. . .Men scent our fragrance on the air,
Yet take no heed
Of humble lessons we would read.

The love of God accomplishes all things quietly
and completely; it is not anxious or uncertain.

LILIAN WHITING

But not alone the fairest flowers:
The merest grass
Along the roadside where we pass. . .

Where others see but the dawn coming. . .I see the soul of God shouting for joy.

WILLIAM BLAKE

. . .Tell of His love who sends the dew,
The rain and sunshine too,
To nourish one small seed.

In all things count on God—
who does not change.

Hope Clark

The violets whisper from the shade
Which their own leaves have made. . .

When my battles are successful, Lord, it is because You have gone with me. In my own strength, I have no power over my enemies; only Your hand can save me. Amen.

. . .Men scent our fragrance on the air,
Yet take no heed
Of humble lessons we would read.

You are my hiding place; you will protect me from
trouble and surround me with songs of deliverance.

PSALM 32:7 NIV

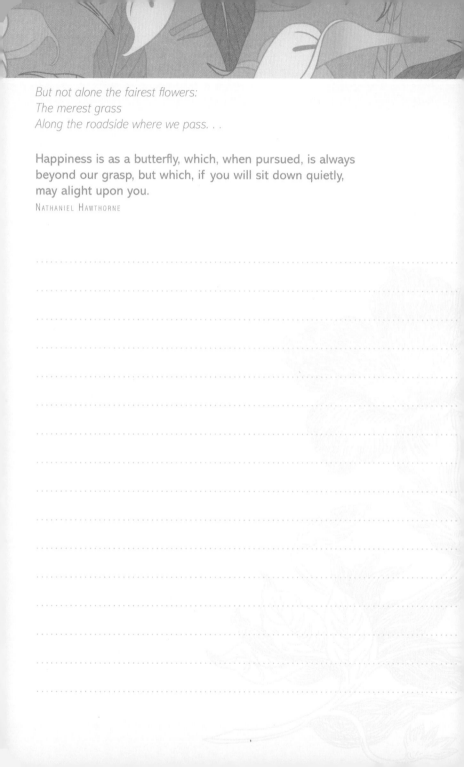

But not alone the fairest flowers:
The merest grass
Along the roadside where we pass. . .

Happiness is as a butterfly, which, when pursued, is always
beyond our grasp, but which, if you will sit down quietly,
may alight upon you.

NATHANIEL HAWTHORNE

. . .Tell of His love who sends the dew,
The rain and sunshine too,
To nourish one small seed.

Set your thoughts, not on the storm,
but on the Love that rules the storm.

MRS. CHARLES E. COWMAN

The violets whisper from the shade
Which their own leaves have made. . .

God writes the gospel not in the Bible
alone, but on trees and flowers and
clouds and stars.
MARTIN LUTHER

. . . .

. . . .

. . . .

. . . .

. . . .

. . . .

. . . .

. . . .

. . . .

. . . .

. . . .

. . . .

. . . .

. . . .

. . . .

. . .Men scent our fragrance on the air,
Yet take no heed
Of humble lessons we would read.

I know that as a Christian I need not fear the
storms of life. When I feel afraid, help me to
focus my eyes on You, Lord. Amen.

But not alone the fairest flowers:
The merest grass
Along the roadside where we pass. . .

I will say of the LORD, "He is
my refuge and my fortress,
my God, in whom I trust."

PSALM 91:2 NIV

. . .Tell of His love who sends the dew,
The rain and sunshine too,
To nourish one small seed.

Hope is like the sun, which,
as we journey toward it,
casts the shadow of our burden behind us.

SAMUEL SMILES

The violets whisper from the shade
Which their own leaves have made. . .

In all ranks of life the human heart yearns for the
beautiful; and the beautiful things that
God makes are His gift to all alike.

HARRIET BEECHER STOWE

. . .Men scent our fragrance on the air,
Yet take no heed
Of humble lessons we would read.

Hope is not a granted wish or a favor performed;
no, it is far greater than that. It is a zany, unpredictable
dependence on a God who loves to surprise us out
of our socks.

MAX LUCADO

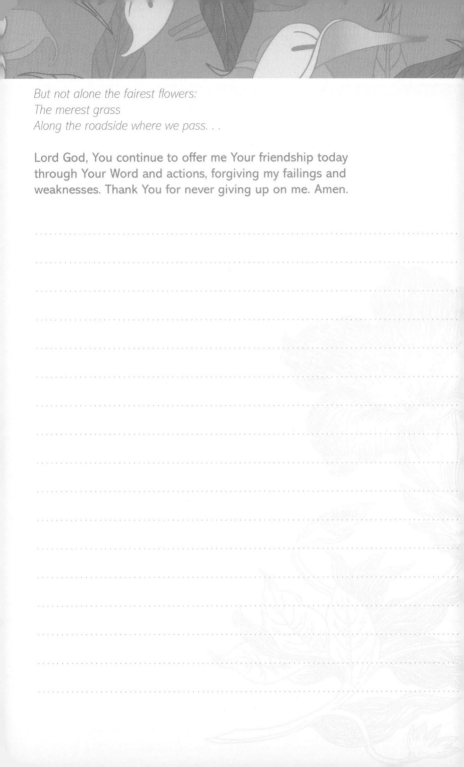

But not alone the fairest flowers:
The merest grass
Along the roadside where we pass. . .

Lord God, You continue to offer me Your friendship today through Your Word and actions, forgiving my failings and weaknesses. Thank You for never giving up on me. Amen.

. . .Tell of His love who sends the dew,
The rain and sunshine too,
To nourish one small seed.

"In quietness and confidence shall be your strength."
ISAIAH 30:15 NKJV

The violets whisper from the shade
Which their own leaves have made. . .

All our actions take their hue from the
complexion of the heart, as landscapes
their variety from light.
Francis Bacon

....
....
....
....
....
....
....
....
....
....
....
....
....
....
....
....
....

. . .Men scent our fragrance on the air,
Yet take no heed
Of humble lessons we would read.

In waiting we begin to get in touch with
the rhythms of life. . . . They are the
rhythms of God. It is in the everyday and
the commonplace that we learn patience,
acceptance, and contentment.

RICHARD J. FOSTER

But not alone the fairest flowers:
The merest grass
Along the roadside where we pass. . .

Serenity is active. It is a gentle and firm participation with trust.

ANNE WILSON SCHAEF

. . .Tell of His love who sends the dew,
The rain and sunshine too,
To nourish one small seed.

My soul flourishes, Lord, like a
well-watered garden carefully tended by Your
hand. Thank You for nourishing my life
and making it fruitful. Amen.

The violets whisper from the shade
Which their own leaves have made. . .

The steadfast love of the Lord never ceases,
his mercies never come to an end;
they are new every morning; great is your faithfulness.

LAMENTATIONS 3:22–23 NRSV

. . .Men scent our fragrance on the air,
Yet take no heed
Of humble lessons we would read.

I love tranquil solitude
And such society
As is quiet, wise, and good.
PERCY BYSSHE SHELLEY

But not alone the fairest flowers:
The merest grass
Along the roadside where we pass. . .

This is my Father's world: He shines in all that's fair;
In the rustling grass I hear Him pass;
He speaks to me everywhere.

MALTBIE D. BABCOCK

. . .Tell of His love who sends the dew,
The rain and sunshine too,
To nourish one small seed.

Be patient with everyone, but above all with thyself.
I mean, do not be disheartened by your imperfections,
but always rise up with fresh courage.

FRANCIS DE SALES

The violets whisper from the shade
Which their own leaves have made. . .

Thank You, Father God, for the fruit You
have given me through the years. When
I live to serve You through worship and
obedience, I do not wither or faint. Amen.

. . .Men scent our fragrance on the air,
Yet take no heed
Of humble lessons we would read.

I lift up my eyes to the hills—where does my
help come from? My help comes from the
LORD, the Maker of heaven and earth.

PSALM 121:1–2 NIV

But not alone the fairest flowers:
The merest grass
Along the roadside where we pass. . .

**The more I study nature, the more
I am amazed at the Creator.**

Louis Pasteur

. . .Tell of His love who sends the dew,
The rain and sunshine too,
To nourish one small seed.

The patterns of our days are always
changing. . .rearranging. . .and each
design for living is unique. . .graced
with its own special beauty.

UNKNOWN

The violets whisper from the shade
Which their own leaves have made. . .

Each little flower that opens, each little
bird that sings, God made their glowing
colors, He made their tiny wings.

CECIL FRANCES ALEXANDER

. . .Men scent our fragrance on the air,
Yet take no heed
Of humble lessons we would read.

Lord, help me to trust in Your words and put
them to work in my life. When I am reminded of
my past, help me drop the memory of that sin
into the ocean of Your love. Amen.

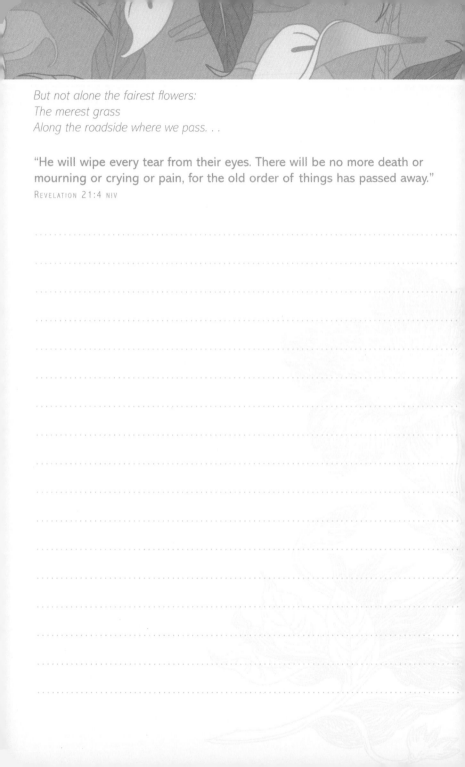

But not alone the fairest flowers:
The merest grass
Along the roadside where we pass. . .

"He will wipe every tear from their eyes. There will be no more death or mourning or crying or pain, for the old order of things has passed away."
REVELATION 21:4 NIV

. . .Tell of His love who sends the dew,
The rain and sunshine too,
To nourish one small seed.

The wonder of living is held within the beauty of silence,
the glory of sunlight, the sweetness of fresh spring air,
the quiet strength of earth, and the love that lies
at the very root of all things.

UNKNOWN

The violets whisper from the shade
Which their own leaves have made. . .

Happy is he who yields himself
completely. . .to God.
François Fénelon

. . .Men scent our fragrance on the air,
Yet take no heed
Of humble lessons we would read.

To be alive, to be able to see, to walk,
to have a home. . .friends—it's all a miracle.
I have adopted the technique of living
life from miracle to miracle.

ARTHUR RUBENSTEIN

But not alone the fairest flowers:
The merest grass
Along the roadside where we pass. . .

O Father, You have given me all I need
to live a joyful life, and I rejoice in Your
gifts of beauty. Amen.

. . .Tell of His love who sends the dew,
The rain and sunshine too,
To nourish one small seed.

The LORD is my light and my salvation—
whom shall I fear?

PSALM 27:1 NIV

The violets whisper from the shade
Which their own leaves have made. . .

I have learned to live each day as it comes,
and not to borrow trouble by dreading tomorrow.

DOROTHY DIX

. . .Men scent our fragrance on the air,
Yet take no heed
Of humble lessons we would read.

Attaining inner simplicity is learning to live happily
in the present moment. Keep in mind that life is a
continuous succession of present moments.

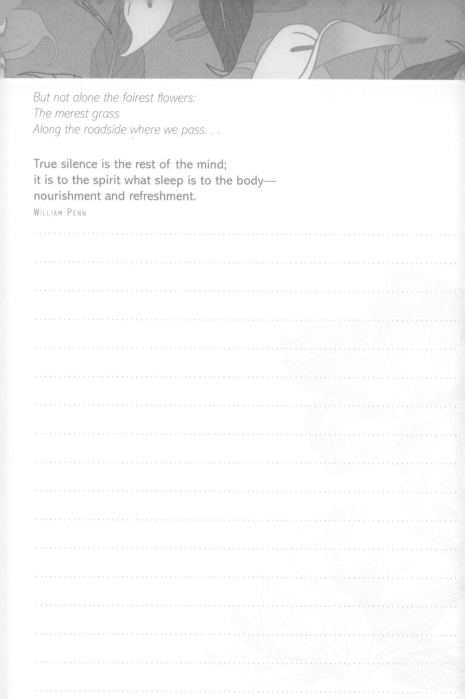

But not alone the fairest flowers:
The merest grass
Along the roadside where we pass. . .

True silence is the rest of the mind;
it is to the spirit what sleep is to the body—
nourishment and refreshment.
WILLIAM PENN

. . .Tell of His love who sends the dew,
The rain and sunshine too,
To nourish one small seed.

Lord. . .open my heart and show me where I am needed,
and I will trust the rest to You. Amen.

The violets whisper from the shade
Which their own leaves have made. . .

May God himself, the God of peace,
sanctify you through and through.
1 THESSALONIANS 5:23 NIV

. . . .

. . . .

. . . .

. . . .

. . . .

. . . .

. . . .

. . . .

. . . .

. . . .

. . . .

. . . .

. . . .

. . . .

. . .Men scent our fragrance on the air,
Yet take no heed
Of humble lessons we would read.

Never lose an opportunity of seeing
anything that is beautiful; for beauty is God's
handwriting—a wayside sacrament.
Welcome it in every fair sky, in every fair flower,
and thank God for it as a cup of blessing.

RALPH WALDO EMERSON

But not alone the fairest flowers:
The merest grass
Along the roadside where we pass. . .

I'll tell you how the sun rose—
one ribbon at a time.

EMILY DICKINSON

. . .Tell of His love who sends the dew,
The rain and sunshine too,
To nourish one small seed.

The true home of a Christian is in the
heavenly realm with Christ and in a
body of immortality and glory.

PETER TOON

The violets whisper from the shade
Which their own leaves have made. . .

No matter how I strive to live righteously, Lord,
I will always fall short of Your standards.
Thank You for making my perfection possible
in the life to come. By myself, I would certainly fail.
With You, anything is possible. Amen.

. . .Men scent our fragrance on the air,
Yet take no heed
Of humble lessons we would read.

Fix your thoughts on what is true, and honorable,
and right, and pure, and lovely, and admirable.
Think about things that are excellent and worthy of
praise. . . . Then the God of peace will be with you.

PHILIPPIANS 4:8—9 NLT

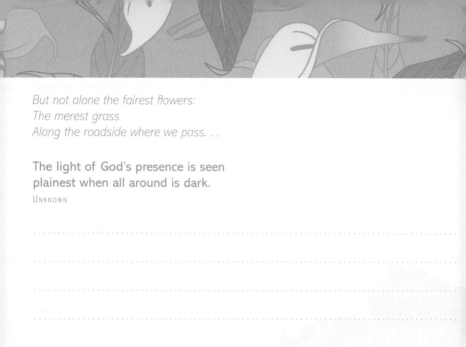

But not alone the fairest flowers:
The merest grass
Along the roadside where we pass. . .

**The light of God's presence is seen
plainest when all around is dark.**
Unknown

. . .Tell of His love who sends the dew,
The rain and sunshine too,
To nourish one small seed.

Pray now; draw on the grace of God in
[your] moment of need.

OSWALD CHAMBERS

The violets whisper from the shade
Which their own leaves have made. . .

All that is good, all that is true, all that is beautiful, all that is beneficent, be it great or small, be it perfect or fragmentary, natural as well as supernatural, moral as well as material, comes from God.

JOHN NEWMAN

. . .*Men scent our fragrance on the air,*
Yet take no heed
Of humble lessons we would read.

A long lifetime of experience brings wisdom
that should be shared. Keep my heart young
and my spirit strong, Father, so I may do
Your work throughout my life. Amen.

But not alone the fairest flowers:
The merest grass
Along the roadside where we pass. . .

The LORD is my strength and my shield;
my heart trusted in him,
and I am helped.

PSALM 28:7 KJV

. . .Tell of His love who sends the dew,
The rain and sunshine too,
To nourish one small seed.

If you surrender completely to the moments as they pass,
you live more richly those moments.

ANNE MORROW LINDBERG

The violets whisper from the shade
Which their own leaves have made. . .

The best thing to give your enemy is forgiveness;
to an opponent, tolerance; to a friend, your heart;
to your child, a good example. . .
to yourself, respect; to all. . .charity.

LORD BALFOUR

. . .Men scent our fragrance on the air,
Yet take no heed
Of humble lessons we would read.

I asked God for all things that I may enjoy life.
He gave me life that I might enjoy all things.
UNKNOWN

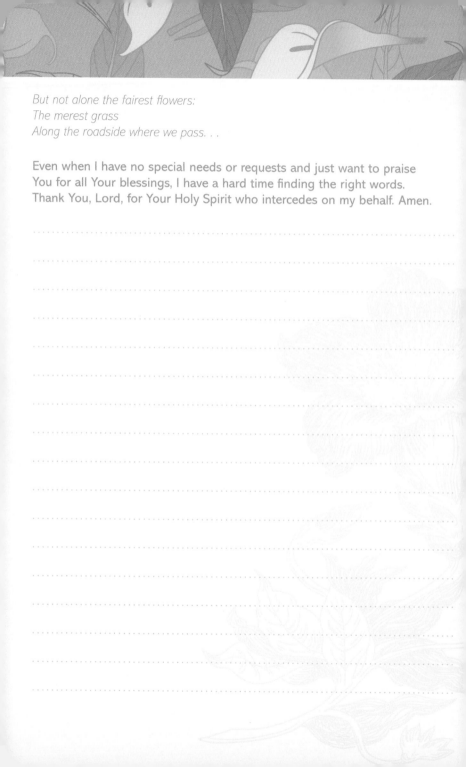

But not alone the fairest flowers:
The merest grass
Along the roadside where we pass. . .

Even when I have no special needs or requests and just want to praise
You for all Your blessings, I have a hard time finding the right words.
Thank You, Lord, for Your Holy Spirit who intercedes on my behalf. Amen.

. . .Tell of His love who sends the dew,
The rain and sunshine too,
To nourish one small seed.

Now the God of hope fill you with all joy and peace in
believing, that ye may abound in hope.

ROMANS 15:13 KJV

The violets whisper from the shade
Which their own leaves have made. . .

Between the house and the store there are little
pockets of happiness. A bird, a garden, a friend's
greeting, a child's smile, a cat in the sunshine
needing a stroke. Recognize them or ignore them.
It's always up to you.

PAM BROWN

. . . .

. . . .

. . . .

. . . .

. . . .

. . . .

. . . .

. . . .

. . . .

. . . .

. . . .

. . . .

. . . .

. . . .

. . . .

. . .Men scent our fragrance on the air,
Yet take no heed
Of humble lessons we would read.

Let nothing disturb you; let nothing
frighten you: Everything passes away
except God; God alone is sufficient.

TERESA OF AVILA

But not alone the fairest flowers:
The merest grass
Along the roadside where we pass. . .

I believe that in each little thing
created by God there is more than
what is understood.

TERESA OF AVILA

. . .Tell of His love who sends the dew,
The rain and sunshine too,
To nourish one small seed.

I tell You my problems and You listen,
Lord. I speak of the good things in my
life and You smile. I ask You for advice,
knowing it will come in Your time.
I am no longer lonely; I am loved. Amen.

The violets whisper from the shade
Which their own leaves have made. . .

If I go up to the heavens, you are there;
if I make my bed in the depths, you are there.
If I rise on the wings of the dawn, if I settle on
the far side of the sea, even there your hand
will guide me, your right hand will hold me fast.

PSALM 139:8–10 NIV

. . .Men scent our fragrance on the air,
Yet take no heed
Of humble lessons we would read.

It's not what you look at that matters;
it's what you see.

HENRY DAVID THOREAU

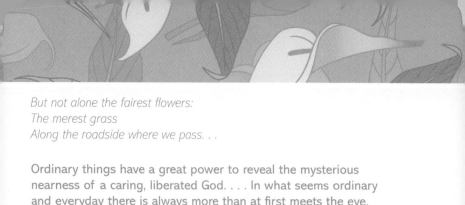

But not alone the fairest flowers:
The merest grass
Along the roadside where we pass. . .

Ordinary things have a great power to reveal the mysterious
nearness of a caring, liberated God. . . . In what seems ordinary
and everyday there is always more than at first meets the eye.
CHARLES CUMMINGS

. . .Tell of His love who sends the dew,
The rain and sunshine too,
To nourish one small seed.

The riches that are in the heart cannot be stolen.
RUSSIAN PROVERB

The violets whisper from the shade
Which their own leaves have made...

Thank You for Your care for each
of Your children, Lord. I will turn
my heart to You for provision
for my body and soul. Amen.

. . .Men scent our fragrance on the air,
Yet take no heed
Of humble lessons we would read.

I have loved you with an everlasting
love; therefore I have continued
my faithfulness to you.

JEREMIAH 31:3 NRSV

But not alone the fairest flowers:
The merest grass
Along the roadside where we pass. . .

Some gifts are big, others are small.
Gifts from the heart are
the best gifts of all.

UNKNOWN

. . .Tell of His love who sends the dew,
The rain and sunshine too,
To nourish one small seed.

God doesn't want us to know the future;
He wants us to know Him.
He wants us to trust Him to guide us into
the future one step at a time.

<small>STORMIE OMARTIAN</small>

The violets whisper from the shade
Which their own leaves have made. . .

Seeing our Father in everything makes life one
long thanksgiving and gives a rest of heart.

HANNAH WHITALL SMITH

. . .Men scent our fragrance on the air,
Yet take no heed
Of humble lessons we would read.

Heavenly Father, You have blessed me with abundant life.
My life with You is full. I don't ever want it to end—and
I'm grateful that it never will. I will spend eternity with You.
Amen.

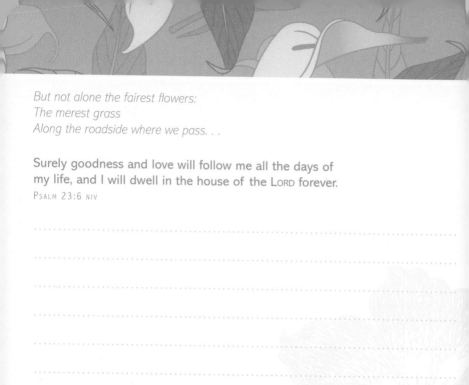

But not alone the fairest flowers:
The merest grass
Along the roadside where we pass. . .

Surely goodness and love will follow me all the days of
my life, and I will dwell in the house of the LORD forever.
PSALM 23:6 NIV

. . .Tell of His love who sends the dew,
The rain and sunshine too,
To nourish one small seed.

In His arms
He carries us all day long

FANNY CROSBY

The violets whisper from the shade
Which their own leaves have made. . .

**The key to happiness belongs to everyone
on earth who recognizes simple things
as treasures of great worth.**
UNKNOWN

. . .Men scent our fragrance on the air,
Yet take no heed
Of humble lessons we would read.

Plant kindness and gather love.

UNKNOWN